SYLLABUBS AND FRUIT FOOLS

ELIZABETH DAVID

Published in 2023 by
Grub Street
4 Rainham Close
London
SW11 6SS

Email: food@grubstreet.co.uk
Twitter: @grub_street
Facebook: Grub Street Publishing
Instagram: grubstreetpublishinguk
Web: www.grubstreet.co.uk

ISBN 978-1-911667-08-7

Printed and bound by Print Best, Estonia

Publishers note: The four booklets which constitute this set were first published by
Elizabeth David Ltd for sale in her shop Kitchen Utensils, 46 Bourne Street, London
SW1 in 1968 and 1969. They are reissued using the original texts which have not
been updated.

CONTENTS

SYLLABUB

It was Herbert Beerbohm Tree's wedding day. His halfbrother had been called in to act as best man in place of his real brother who had vanished to Spain. At the celebration breakfast there were syllabubs. Herbert was beguiled by the biblical rhythm of the name. 'And Sillabub, the son of Sillabub reigned in his stead' he intoned. His stepbrother, half-scandalised and wholly impressed by Herbert's levity, never forgot the episode. He had been ten years old at the time of Herbert's wedding; his name was Max Beerbohm; the story is recounted in Lord David Cecil's *Max, a Biography*[1]; the date was 1882, and sillabub[2], added Max, was then his favourite dish.

Max Beerbohm's generation must have been the last to which the delicious syllabub was a familiar childhood treat. Already for nearly a century the syllabub had been keeping company with the trifle, and in due course the trifle came to reign in the syllabub's stead; and before long the party pudding of the English was not any more the fragile whip of cream contained in a little glass, concealing within its innocent white froth a powerful alcoholic punch, but a built-up confection of sponge fingers and ratafias soaked in wine and brandy,

1 Published by Constable, 1964

2 The spelling is Max Beerbohm's

spread with jam, clothed in an egg-and-cream custard, topped with a syllabub and strewn with little coloured comfits. Came 1846, the year that Mr. Alfred Bird brought forth custard powder; and Mr. Bird's brain-child grew and grew until all the land was covered with custard made with custard powder and the Trifle had become custard's favourite resting-place. The wine and lemon-flavoured cream whip or syllabub which had crowned the Trifle had begun to disappear. Sponge cake left over from millions of nursery teas usurped the place of sponge fingers and the little bitter almond macaroons called ratafias. Kitchen sherry replaced Rhenish and Madeira and Lisbon wines. Brandy was banished. The little coloured comfits – sugar-coated coriander seeds and caraways – bright as tiny tiddlywinks, went into a decline and in their stead reigned candied angelica and nicely varnished glace cherries.

Now seeking means to combat the Chemicals Age, we look to our forbears for help. We find that the syllabub can replace the synthetic ice cream which replaced the trifle which replaced the syllabub in the first place. The ingredients of a syllabub, we find, are simple and sumptuous. The skill demanded for its confection is minimal, the presentation is basic and elegant. Swiftly, now, before the deep-freezers, the dehydrators and the emulsifiers take the syllabub away from us and return it transformed and forever despoiled, let us discover how it was made in its heyday and what we can do to recapture something of its pristine charm.

In the beginning then, in the 17th and 18th centuries, there were three kinds of syllabub. There was the syllabub mixed in a punch bowl on a basis of cider or ale and sometimes both, sweetened with sugar and spiced with cinnamon or nutmeg. Into the bowl the milkmaid milked the cow so that the new warm milk fell in a foam and froth on to the cider. The contents of the bowl were left undisturbed for an hour or two, by which time a kind of honeycombed curd had formed on the top, leaving alcoholic whey underneath. Sometimes, on top of the milk curd, a layer of thick fresh cream was poured. This syllabub was more a drink than a whip, a diversion for country parties and rustic festivals.

Co-existing with the syllabub of pastoral England was one made with wine and spirits instead of cider and ale, and with cream instead of milk. This mixture was a more solid one. It was about four-fifths sweetened whipped cream, to be spooned rather than drunk out of the glasses in which it was served, and one fifth of wine and whey which had separated from the whip, and which you drank when you reached the end of the cream. Then, at some stage, it was discovered that by reducing the proportions of wine and sugar to cream, the whip would remain thick and light without separating. This version was called a solid or everlasting syllabub. One 18th century author, E. Smith, whose *Complete Housewife* published in 1727, was also the first cookery book to be printed in America, claimed that her Everlasting Syllabubs would remain in perfect condition for nine or ten days, although at their best after three or four.

Not all syllabubs were necessarily made with wine. Sir Kenelm Digby, whose book of recipes collected from his contemporaries and friends has provided posterity with a graphic record of Stuart cookery, notes that he himself made a fine syllabub with syrup left over from the home-drying of plums; being 'very quick of the fruit and very weak of sugar' this syrup 'makes the Syllabub exceeding well tasted' says Sir Kenelm. He adds that cherry syrup may be used in like manner. In the 18th and 19th centuries, syllabubs were sometimes made with the juice of Seville oranges, and in these days we can devise cream and wine or cream and fruit-syrup syllabubs to suit ourselves.

Before venturing on new formulas, however, it is as well to have an idea of what the old recipes were like and to know in what quantities, approximately, the ingredients were portioned out. From the following cross-section of recipes, chosen from cookery books written by professional and practising cooks and from household receipt books of the 17th, 18th and 19th centuries, emerges a fairly clear picture of the ways in which the cooks of the Stuart, the Georgian and the Victorian eras made and served their syllabubs. Historical and documentary interest apart, some of the old recipes are remarkable for the beauty and the clarity of the English in which they are written.

THE SEVENTEENTH CENTURY

AN EXCELLENT SYLLABUB. 'Fill your Sillabub pot half full with sider, and good store of sugar, and a little nutmeg, stir it well together, and put in as much cream by two or three spoonfuls at a time, as hard as you can, as though you milk it in; then stir it together very softly once about, and let it stand two hours before you eat it, for the standing makes it curd.'

Robert May. *The Accomplisht Cook*, 1660.

The author of this celebrated Stuart cookery book was a professional cook whose father, also a professional, apprenticed him to Arthur Hollingsworth, cook and caterer to one of the City Guilds during the last years of the 16th century. Since May was seventy-two when his book was published, it is clear that many of his recipes must date back to the days of Queen Elizabeth.

A SYLLABUB. 'My Lady Middlesex makes Syllabubs for little glasses with spouts, thus. Take three pints of Sweet Cream, one of quick white wine (or Rhenish[3]) and a good wine glassful (better the

---

3 Rhine wine

¼ of a pint) of Sack[4]: mingle with them about three quarters of a pound of fine Sugar in Powder.

Beat all these together with a whisk, till all appeareth converted into froth, and let them stand all night. The next day the Curd will be thick and firm above, and the drink clear under it. I conceive it may do well, to put into each glass (when you pour the liquor into it) a sprig of Rosemary a little bruised, or a little Limon-peel, or some such thing to quicken the taste; or use Amber-sugar, or spirit of Cinnamon, or of LignumCassie[5], or Nutmegs, or Mace, or Cloves, a very little.'

The Closet of the Eminently Learned Sir Kenelme Digby Kt. Opened
Published by his Son's Consent 1669.

Sir Kenelm Digby, philosopher-scientist, soldier-diplomat, ardent royalist, lifelong friend and confidant of Charles the First's widow, Queen Henrietta Maria, was born in 1603 and died in 1663. His recipes, some his own and many collected from his friends and contemporaries, were put together in the form of a private notebook rather than for publication. They provide us with a firsthand and unique record of cooking as it was understood and practised in the kitchens and still-rooms of aristocratic houses of the first half of the 17th century.

---

4 Sherry

5 Cassia bark, an alternative to cinnamon, cheaper and less pungent

THE
EIGHTEENTH CENTURY

TO MAKE WHIPT SYLLABUBS. 'Take a quart of Creme and a pint of rhenish wine and the juice of 4 lemons sweeten it to your taste and put in some leamon peele then whip it up with a small rod and put it with a spoone into syllabub glasses.'

The MS. receipt book of Judith Frampton of Morton House, nr. Dorchester, Dorset. 1708. Quoted in *Dorset Dishes of the 18th Century*, edited by J. Stevens Cox, published by the Dorset Natural History and Archaelogical Society, Dorchester 1961.

TO MAKE LEMON SYLLABUB. 'To a pint of cream put a pound of double-refined sugar, the juice of seven lemons, grate the rinds of two lemons into a pint of white wine, add half a pint of sack, then put them all into a deep pot, and whisk them for half an hour, put it into glasses the night before you want it: it is better for standing two or three days, but it will keep a week if required.'

Elizabeth Raffald. *The Experienced English Housekeeper*, 1769.

Elizabeth Raffald was a Yorkshire woman, housekeeper in the Cheshire household of Lady Elizabeth Warburton. She married

Lady Elizabeth's head gardener, left her service to run a catering establishment in Manchester, bore sixteen daughters, and managed the kitchens in two different Manchester inns. Her book, substantially as she wrote it, was still in print, and selling, a hundred years after its original publication.

A FINE SYLLABUB FROM THE COW. 'Sweeten a quart of cyder with refined sugar, grate a nutmeg over it; and milk the cow into your liquor. When you have added what is necessary, pour half-a-pint of the sweetest cream over it.'

Barbara Young, Steyning, Sussex. MS. receipt book, 1781. From *Dorset Dishes of the 18th Century*, already quoted on page 9.

THE NINETEENTH CENTURY

SOMERSETSHIRE SYLLABUB. 'Sweeten a pint of port, and another of Madeira or sherry, in a china bowl. Milk about three pints of milk over this. In a short time it will bear clouted cream laid over it. Grate nutmeg over this, and strew a few coloured comfits on the top if you choose.'

Mistress Margaret Dods. *The Cook's and Housewife's Manual*, 4th edition 1829.

The copious footnotes to the recipes in this book were believed by his contemporaries to have been written by Sir Walter Scott. Margaret or Meg Dods is a character in Scott's *St. Ronan's Well*. It was also the pseudonym used by Christina Jane Johnstone, wife of an Edinburgh publisher. Her cookery book is still one of the two main sources of authentic Scottish recipes. The other is *The Scots Kitchen*, a fine book by a living writer, Marian McNeill. *The Scots Kitchen* was first published by Blackie and Son in 1929.

THE TWENTIETH CENTURY

My own version of Everlasting Syllabub.

One small glass, or 4 oz, of white wine or sherry, 2 tablespoons of brandy, one lemon, 2 oz of sugar, ½ pint of double cream, nutmeg.

The day before the syllabub is to be made, put the thinly pared rind of the lemon and the juice in a bowl with the wine and brandy and leave overnight. Next day, strain the wine and lemon mixture into a large and deep bowl. Add the sugar and stir until it has dissolved. Pour in the cream slowly, stirring all the time. Grate in a little nutmeg. Now whisk the mixture until it thickens and will hold a soft peak on the whisk. The process may take 5 minutes, it may take as long as 15. It depends on the cream, the temperature and the method of whisking. Unless dealing with a large quantity of cream, an electric mixer can be perilous. A couple of seconds too long and the cream is a ruined and grainy mass. For a small amount of cream a wire whisk is perfectly satisfactory and just as quick as an electric beater. An old-fashioned wooden chocolate mill or whisk held upright and twirled between the palms of both hands is also a good implement for whisking cream. The important point is to learn to recognise the moment at which the whisking process is complete.

When the cream is ready, spoon it into glasses, which should be of very small capacity (2 to 2½ oz) but filled to overflowing. Once in the glasses the cream will not spoil nor sink nor separate. A tiny sprig of rosemary or a little twist of lemon peel can, as suggested by Sir Kenelm Digby, be stuck into each little filled glass. Keep the syllabubs in a cool place – not in the refrigerator – until you are ready to serve them. They can be made at least two days before they are needed. The quantities given will fill ten small syllabub or custard cups or sherry glasses and will be enough for four to six people. Though circumstances are so changed it is relevant to remember that in their heyday syllabubs were regarded as refreshments to be offered at card parties, ball suppers and at public entertainments, rather than just as a pudding for lunches and dinners.

For those interested in tracing the evolution of our national dishes, the brief recipe on page 30 shows how the syllabub and the trifle were eventually amalgamated to make one glorious sticky mess. Then, looking back into the old recipes for English fruit fools, we find that trifles, syllabubs, creams and fools have all at some point merged one with the other. In the history of cookery nothing is conveniently consistent.

ENGLISH FRUIT FOOLS

Our frailties are invincible

Robert Louis Stevenson.

Soft, pale, creamy, untroubled, the English fruit fool is the most frail and insubstantial of English summer dishes. That at any rate is how it should be, and how we like to think it always was. Here the old cookery books interrupt the smooth sequence. The seventeenth and eighteenth century writers do describe a number of fruit fools, fools made from gooseberries, raspberries, strawberries, redcurrants, apples, mulberries, apricots, even from fresh figs; but few of these dishes turn out to be the simple cream-enriched purées we know today. Some were made from rather roughly crushed fruit (the French word *foule*, meaning crushed or pressed must surely have some bearing on the English name) often they were thickened with eggs as well as cream, sometimes they were flavoured with wine and spices, perfumed sugar and lemon peel.

Two hundred years ago it was those recipes listed under the heading of creams which were much more like the fruit fools of today. Evidently, at some stage, it came to be appreciated that the eggs and the extra flavourings were unnecessary, that they even distort the fresh flavour of the fruit. This is especially true of berry fruits and of apricots. Gradually the delicacy now regarded as the traditional English fruit fool came to be accepted as a purée of fruit plus sugar, fresh thick cream, and nothing more.

Like the syllabub, the fruit fool was almost always served in glasses or custard cups, although Susannah MacIver, an Edinburgh cookery teacher and author of an excellent little book called *Cookery and Pastry*, 1774, directs that her gooseberry cream be served on an 'asset', the old Scots word for platter.

From the following few recipes it is easy to see that there was never any one method of making English fruit creams and fools, and that over the past three centuries the two have fused. In the process some charming variations have disappeared. Some of these would be worth reviving, for example Elizabeth Hammond's gooseberry or apple trifle quoted on page 19 and Robert May's beautiful 'black fruit' mixtures.

In this selection of old and modern recipes I give precedence to those dishes made from the gooseberry, because green gooseberry fool is – to me at any rate – the most delicious as well as the most characteristic of all these simple, almost childlike, English dishes.

GOOSEBERRY FOOL

This is my own method of making gooseberry fool.

2 lb of green gooseberries; ½ lb of sugar; a minimum of ½ pint of double cream.

Wash the gooseberries. There is no need to top and tail them. Put them into the top half of a double saucepan with the sugar, and steam them (or if it is easier bake them in a covered jar in a low oven) until they are quite soft. Sieve them through the mouli having first strained off surplus liquid which would make the fool watery. When the purée is quite cold add the cream. More sugar may be necessary.

Later in the season when gooseberries are over, delicious fools can be made with uncooked strawberries; a mixture of raspberries and redcurrants, also uncooked; and blackberries, cooked as for gooseberries; but in this case I think that cream spoils the rich colour of the fruit and should be offered separately.

To me it is essential to serve fruit fools in glasses or in simple white cups, and with shortbread or other such biscuits to go with them.

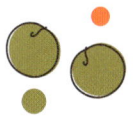

ICED GOOSEBERRY FOOL

'1 quart green gooseberries; ½ lb white sugar; 1 pint of whipped cream; brandy or maraschino; vegetable greening; a little water; grated lemon peel.'

'Stew very slowly one quart of green gooseberries with half a pound of white sugar and enough water to prevent fruit from burning. Rub through a hair sieve and use a very little vegetable greening to make it a pretty colour. (Add brandy or maraschino if required.) One pint of cream whipped stiff and grated lemon peel. Mix well together and freeze. Should take two hours to freeze and should be worked with a wooden spoon from time to time.'

Ruth Lowinsky. *Lovely Food, a Cookery Notebook.*
Nonesuch Press, London 1931.

I find this recipe most interesting. The thirties was the decade when smart hostesses took to serving a great many dishes iced or frozen simply for the originality of the idea. In England at this time it was quite avant garde to possess a refrigerator. Iced camembert cream, frozen horseradish sauce, and tomato ice all belong to this period. I remember a cook of my childhood whose great dish was a crème brûlée in which the layer of glass-like caramel concealed not the usual egg-thickened cream, but a delicate and softly frozen gooseberry fool.

Ruth Lowinsky's book is a true period piece, which is to say that in its time it was bang up to date. The recipes and the suggested menus evoke the days of English parlourmaids handing round every course in silver-plated entrée dishes far too big for the food they contained, while the illustrations of table decorations devised by Mr. Thomas Lowinsky depict such conversation stimulators as 'two dead branches in an accumulator jar', or 'a spiral of chromium-plated steel pierced with holes through which the stems of flowers are passed'. Today's equivalents do not adorn our tables. They are worn by our guests. The clanking camisoles and the chain mail adornments of the sixties are certainly less static than the table decorations of the thirties; they exist surely for the same reason, to invite comment.

In sharp contrast the redundant vegetable greening and liqueurs in Mrs. Lowinsky's gooseberry fool recipe hark back to Hannah Glasse and the mid-eighteenth century. Hannah Glasse's book, *The Art of Cookery Made Plain and Easy* was first published in 1747; in the 1756 edition appears what is possibly the first English printed recipe for an ice cream. The formula is for a simple raspberry purée and cream mixture which today we should call a raspberry fool. Mrs. Glasse directs that the cream be frozen in 'pewter basons'. What else are our fruit fools but the basis of modern cream ices or frozen desserts?

In the next recipe, the fool has amalgamated with the syllabub *and* the trifle, the gooseberry fool taking the place of the cake at the bottom of the dish. An attractive recipe.

GOOSEBERRY OR APPLE TRIFLE

'Scald a sufficient quantity of fruit, and pulp it through a sieve, add sugar agreeable to taste, make a thick layer of this at the bottom of your dish: mix a pint of milk, a pint of cream, and the yolks of two eggs: scald it over the fire, observing to stir it: add a small quantity of sugar, and let it get cold: then lay it over the apples or gooseberries with a spoon, and put on the whole a whip [a syllabub E.D.] made the day before. If you use apples, add the rind of a lemon grated.'

Elizabeth Hammond. *Modern Domestic Cookery and Useful Receipt Book*, Circa 1817.

The next recipe comes from a work compiled by two eighteenth century London publicans.

TO MAKE GOOSEBERRY FOOL

'Put two quarts of gooseberries into about a quart of water, and set them on the fire. When they begin to simmer, turn yellow, and to plump, throw them into a cullender to drain out the water, and with the back of a spoon carefully squeeze the pulp through a sieve into a dish. Make them pretty sweet, and let them stand till they are cold. In the meantime, take two quarts of milk, and the yolks of four eggs beaten up with a little grated nutmeg. Stir it softly over a slow fire, and when it begins to simmer, take it off, and by degrees stir it into the gooseberries. Let it stand till it be cold, and then serve it up. If you make it with cream, you need not put any eggs.'

Francis Collingwood and John Woollams. *The Universal Cook and City and Country Housekeeper*, 1791.

The main point of interest about the book from which the foregoing recipe is extracted is the French translation which appeared in Paris in 1810.

The flow of English translations from French cookery books has been well-sustained ever since the mid-seventeenth century when La Varenne's celebrated *French Cook* appeared in England. French kitchen terms peppered throughout English cookery books, and half-anglicized names of French dishes are no novelty to us. When for once the tide runs in the reverse direction we get a new view of our own cookery, and a revealing insight into the oddness of traditional names as they appear in another language.

In the case of *Le Cuisinier Anglais Universl ou Le Nec Plus Ultra de la Gourmandise* there are some interesting metemorphoses, as well as signs that the translator was defeated by the names of some of our cherished specialities, among them *le catchup* and *le browning*, ('to even the most skilled of French cooks these sauces will be new', says the publisher's preface). The syllabub turns up as *Eternel Syllabub*, *syllabub solide*, and *syllabub sous la vache*.

La plume of the French translator gives a new aspect to several of our old sweet dishes, among them the trifle which as *bagatelle*, regains something of its lost charm. Cheesecakes also return to grace and elegance as *talmouses*. As for *folie de groseilles vertes* it is no longer perfidious Albion's frailty, serene and cool, but a wild whirl of summer gaiety and greenery.

I fancy that across the channel where Napoleon's wars were ravaging all Europe, our two innkeepers fell flat as pancakes, and were it not for the felicities of their translator they would scarcely be worth comment. All their recipes had been borrowed – by their own admission – from earlier works and their style is charmless. It is a relief to turn back to something with the flavour of originality, an evocation of a truly pastoral summer dish, half fruit fool, half syllabub.

TO MAKE CREAM OF SUNDRY KINDS OF FRUITS

'Take either currants, mulberries, raspberries or strawberries, sprinkle them with a little rose-water; press out the juice, and draw the milk out of the cow's udder into it; sweeten it with a little sugar, and beat it well with birchen twigs, till it froth up; then strew over it a little fine beaten cinamon, and it will be an excellent mess. You may do this with the juice of plums, gooseberries, apricots, figs, or any juicy fruit.'

The Family Magazine Containing Useful Directions in All the Branches of House-keeping and Cookery, 1741.

Now two seventeenth century gooseberry dishes:

TO MAKE GOOSEBERRY CREAM

'Codle them green, and boil them up with sugar, being preserved put them into the cream strain'd or whole scrape sugar on them, and so serve them cold in boil'd or raw cream. Thus you may do strawberries, raspas, or red currans, put in raw cream whole, or serve them with wine and sugar in a dish without cream.'

Robert May. *The Accomplisht Cook*, 1660.

TO MAKE A GOOSEBERRY HUFF

'Take a quart of green gooseberries boil them and pulp them thro' a sieve, take the whites of 3 eggs, beat them to a Froth, put it to the Gooseberries and beat it both together till it looks white, then take ½ pound refin'd sugar, make it into a Syrrup with Spring Water, boyl it to a Candy, [i.e. to the small thread [E.D.] let it be almost cold then put it to the Gooseberries and Eggs and beat all toghether till tis all froth, which put into Cup or Glasses – Codlings [green apples [E.D.] may be done the same way.'

N.B. Eleven Ounces of Codlin pulp'd thro' a sieve is a proper quantity to the above Eggs and Sugar.'

Dorset Dishes of the 17th Century. Edited from MS. receipt books and published by J. Stevens Cox. The Toucan Press, Guernsey, 1967.

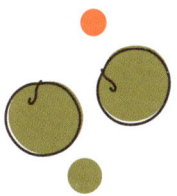

BLACK FRUIT FOOL OR BLACK TART STUFF

This is a recipe adapted from a dish evidently popular three hundred years ago in the days of the Stuarts, when a purée of dried prunes, raisins and currants cooked in wine was used as a filling for tarts and pies. Recipes for this 'black tart stuff' as it was called appear in at least two cookery books of the second half of the 17th century. One of these books, *The Accomplisht Cook* of 1660 has already been quoted on pages 7 and 23. It is a most beautiful piece of cookery literature. The author, Robert May, worked in a number of grand and noble households, including that of the Countess of Kent, whose own receipt book appeared posthumously in 1653 under the title *A True Gentlewoman's Delight*.

Robert May gives several different variations on his 'black tart stuff' recipe, one of which includes damsons. The Countess of Kent's book also gives a formula for black tart stuff. My own version is the result of experiments with these different recipes. I find it a delicious and refreshing cold fruit purée. As a pie filling it is rich and dark without the cloying and heavy qualities of mincemeat. It has also a certain originality which provides a small surprise at the end of the meal.

Exact proportions of the different dried fruits are not important, but as a rough guide, use ½ lb of good large prunes, ½ lb of raisins,

(Spanish muscatels are the best for flavour and colour, stoneless Australian or South African raisins are cheaper) and 2 oz of currants, plus ¼ pint of red table wine or ⅛ pint of port.

Put the prunes in an earthenware oven dish, with the wine and enough water to cover them. Leave them, in the covered pot, in a very slow oven, anything from gas mark ½ to 1 or 290 deg F, to gas 3 or 330 deg F, for 2 to 3 hours or longer, until they are very swollen and completely soft and have absorbed most of the liquid. During the final hour or so of cooking put the raisins and currants previously well washed, in a separate oven pot, and with water to cover them, to bake.

Stone the prunes, sieve them, with any remaining juice. Strain and discard the water from the raisins and currants. Sieve them. Mix the two purées together.

Serve well chilled in glasses, or in one large bowl, with a layer of thin pouring cream floated on the top, and with sponge or shortbread fingers.[6]

When the purée is made a little extra port can be added by those who like a stronger flavour of wine.

These quantities fill six glasses of about 3 oz capacity. The purée keeps well in the refrigerator, so it is economical to make a batch and store it.

A note for teetotallers: I have several times eaten another modern version of this dish in which black coffee rather than wine is used for flavouring the dried fruit.

---

6 See the recipe on page 31

QUINCE FOOL

Quarter and core the quinces but do not peel them; put them in a vegetable steamer – the kind known as an adaptable steamer, which looks a bit like a colander, and fits on the top of the saucepan, *not* a bain marie or double boiler – over a pan of water, and cover them. Steam until they are quite soft. Sieve them. Into the hot pulp stir caster sugar (about 6 to 8 oz for 1½ lb of quinces, but this is a matter of taste). When quite cold fold in about ⅓ to ½ pint of fresh cream.

This is my version of a quince cream recipe from the note book of Mrs. Owen of Penrhos in Wales, 1695.

DRIED APRICOT FOOL

The way to get the maximum flavour out of dried apricots is to bake them slowly in the oven instead of stewing them. They emerge nicely plump, with a roasted, smoky flavour which I find irresistible; although only, it must be said, if they have been dried without the sulphur dioxide used as a preservative for dried fruit. To get good dried apricots it is nowadays necessary to shop for them in wholefood and health-food stores.

Put ½ lb of fine dried apricots to soak in water just to cover for a couple of hours – or overnight if it is more convenient. Cook them, in the same water and without sugar, in a covered oven-pot at a moderate temperature, Gas No. 3, 330 deg F. for about an hour. Strain off the juice. Put the apricots through the coarse mesh of the vegetable mill, and into the resulting purée mix about 4 tablespoons of sugar – the amount depends upon the quality of the apricots as well as upon your own taste – and then stir in about ¼ pint of thick, slightly whipped cream. A good addition to dried apricot fool is a spoonful or two of freshly ground almonds.

Serve chilled in glasses or cups. Enough for four.

RHUBARB FOOL

Rhubarb fool is made in just the same way as gooseberry fool, but needs an even larger proportion of sugar, preferably dark brown, and it is very necessary when the rhubarb is cooked to put it in a colander or sieve and let the excess juice drain off before the purée is made and the cream added.

Rhubarb fool is a very beautiful dish – and to me the only way of making rhubarb acceptable. The brown sugar, incidentally, gives rhubarb a specially rich flavour and colour.

A NINETEENTH CENTURY TRIFLE

'Cover the bottom of the dish with Naples biscuits[7] and macaroons broken in halves, wet with brandy and white wine poured over them, cover them with patches of raspberry jam, fill the dish with a good custard, then whip up a syllabub, drain the froth on a sieve, put it on the custard and strew comfits[8] over all.'

Frederick Bishop. *The Wife's Own Book of Cookery*, 1852.

---

7 At this period a kind of sponge cake cut into fingers. Earlier Naples biscuits were macaroons studded with pine nuts

8 Sugar-coated coriander or caraway seeds

ALMOND SHORTBREAD

A good and simple shortbread to serve with syllabubs, fruit fools, and creams.

3 oz plain flour; 3 oz unsalted butter; 1½ oz of caster sugar; 1 oz of ground almonds; ½ to 1 oz of rice flour or cornflour.

Crumble the softened butter into the flour, sprinkling in the rice flour or cornflour at intervals, as and when the butter seems to be getting sticky. Add the almonds and the sugar.

The ingredients should not be worked too much. Grainy pieces will disappear in the cooking.

Spread the mixture into a six-inch sandwich tin or tart tin with a removable base. Press it down lightly and smooth over the top with a palette knife. Prick the top surface with a fork.

Bake in the centre of a very slow oven, gas No. 2, 310 deg F for an hour and a quarter, until the shortbread is a very pale biscuit colour.

Leave to cool in the tin, but before it is completely cold cut into small neat wedges. Enough for four people.

INDEX OF RECIPES

INDEX OF AUTHORS

THE BAKING OF
AN ENGLISH LOAF

ELIZABETH DAVID

TABLE OF EQUIVALENT OVEN TEMPERATURES

Solid Fuel	Electricity	Gas
Slow	240-310 degrees F / 115-155 degrees C	¼ – 2
Moderate	320-370 degrees F / 160-190 degrees C	3-4
Fairly Hot	380-400 degrees F / 195-205 degrees C	5
Hot	410-440 degrees F / 210-230 degrees C	6-7
Very Hot	450-480 degrees F / 235-250 degrees C	8-9

For Lesley O'Malley

Published in 2023 by
Grub Street
4 Rainham Close
London
SW11 6SS

Email: food@grubstreet.co.uk
Twitter: @grub_street
Facebook: Grub Street Publishing
Instagram: grubstreetpublishinguk
Web: www.grubstreet.co.uk

Text copyright © Elizabeth David 1969, 1970, 1971
The Baking of an English Loaf first published 1969, second impression 1970,
third impression 1971
The Baking of an English Loaf was first published in *Queen* magazine on
December 4, 1968
Copyright this edition © Grub Street 2023
Design: Myriam Bell

ISBN 978-1-911667-08-7

Printed and bound by Print Best, Estonia

Publishers note: The four booklets which constitute this set were first published by
Elizabeth David Ltd for sale in her shop Kitchen Utensils, 46 Bourne Street, London
SW1 in 1968 and 1969. They are reissued using the original texts which have not
been updated.

CONTENTS

THE BAKING OF
AN ENGLISH LOAF

A very exaggerated idea of the difficulty and trouble of bread-making prevails amongst persons who are entirely ignorant of the process

Eliza Acton: *The English Bread Book*, 1857

Any human being possessed of sufficient gumption to track down a source of fresh yeast – it isn't all that rare – and collected enough to remember to buy at the same time a pound or two of plain flour, get it home, take a mixing bowl and a measuring jug from the cupboard and read a few simple instructions can make a decent loaf of bread.

And if you cannot, after two or three attempts, make a *better* loaf than any to be bought in an English shop – and that goes for health-food and whole-food and crank-food and home-spun shops generally, just as much as for chain bakeries and provision stores and small independent bakers – then I am prepared to eat my hat, your hat, and almost anything else put before me, always with the absolute exception of a loaf of English commercial bread.

Please do not jump to conclusions. It is not my intention to make even a slight attempt to persuade you into baking your own bread. I am simply going to tell you how to set about it if you feel you must, and I find it comical as well as shameful that in this day and age anybody should be forced into so archaic an activity.

No Frenchwoman, at least no French townswoman, would dream of baking her own bread. In France, fresh loaves are baked twice daily by every baker and bought twice daily by every householder. If and when the French bakery system breaks down, there is, as every schoolchild knows, a revolution. Had Marie Antoinette been a French princess rather than a Hapsburg from Vienna, she could never have said, or have been credited with saying, that the people of France could make do with cake instead of bread.

As recently as the summer of 1965, the people of Paris rose up in revolt against the annual August closing of some sixty percent of the city's bakeries. To Parisians, it had become a major grievance to be obliged to walk perhaps as far as a kilometre to find a baker who kept his business open during the summer exodus to the sea and the country. The Government was obliged to step in and decree that the bakers (not, mind you, the shoemakers, the plumbers, the electricians, and the laundries, just the bakers) must stagger their holidays. A baker, in other words, has a public responsibility and cannot with impunity desert his post.

In France, a meal without good bread and plenty of it is simply not a meal. For that matter, a meal without bread isn't a meal anywhere in Europe except in England. And I mean England. I do not mean Scotland or Ireland, where it is still possible to buy real bread.

A certain school of English patriot is much given to the expression of belief in the creed that we have in England the finest ingredients in Europe and that "British cuisine at its best is the best in the world".

I find it amazing that any responsible person can presume to make such a claim when our basic necessities are so hard to come by, when a new-laid egg is as rare as a flawless ruby, when English butter is not nearly as well made as Dutch, Danish or Polish, when the best fresh vegetables available to Londoners and other city-dwellers are flown in from Cyprus or Kenya or sent from Italy, Spain or Madeira, when our cheese is marketed by packaging factories, and when, manifestly, not one householder or one restaurateur in a thousand has grasped the elementary truth that the finest ingredients and the greatest cooking skills this side of Escoffier can combine to produce only a bleak and hollow sham of a meal, joyless and devoid of stimulus, if the customer or the guest is offered no more in the way of bread to go with his food than a skimpy little wedge of white winceyette placed with a boarding-house gentility underneath a folded napkin upon a side-plate.

A good many readers of cookery articles must be bored to death with being told that one main dish, with a salad, cheese and a loaf of crusty bread, makes an ample, balanced, nourishing, economical, easily-cooked and satisfying family meal. Well, so it does, if you can get it; in fact, the bread and the cheese would be a perfectly good meal without the so-called main dish. And the bleak truth is that mighty few of us can lay hands on either the cheese or the bread unless we happen to live within walking distance of a specialist cheese shop and a bakery which is not only independent and bakes its own bread but bakes it well and produces it for sale at an hour where the ordinary householder can go out and buy it.

I was driven to making my own bread because my local bakery, which does, in fact, produce quite acceptable French-type loaves, doesn't have them on sale until midday, at which time I, in common with most other women in my neighbourhood, am already busy at the stove preparing lunch and it is highly inconvenient to leave the house. And such is the demand for even remotely edible bread, that if I leave my shopping until the afternoon, nothing but wrapped and sliced factory loaves are left on the baker's shelves.

I repeat, I am not canvassing those who are not prepared to put up with shop bread because they just have not the time or inclination to make it themselves; I am not preaching to those who buy shop bread because they actually like it; I am giving instructions purely as basic guidance to those who have already reached the conclusion that it is pretty ludicrous to spend three days planning menus to include shrimp-filled avocados, trout with almonds, fillet of beef in puff pastry, pineapple ice cream and no end of a palaver over the grinding and percolating of the coffee, if they cannot offer their guests a decent piece of bread. It should be added, in fairness, that in those households where home-made and well-made bread is on offer nobody needs to worry about all that prestige-type food. Have it by all means, if that's what you like, but if it's prestige you're after – or, to put it in a cruder way and since it isn't unknown to any of us occasionally to do the right things for the wrong reasons – what will most impress your friends and arouse the maximum envy in your rivals is the sight and the taste of fresh, authentic, un-cranky bread, with its slightly rough and open texture, plain unvarnished crust, and perceptibly salty bite.

This is the kind of bread which should be cut in good thick chunky slices straight from the loaf left upon the table for all to see and enjoy.

In fact, if I go into a friend's dining-room and see no loaf on the table, I feel as uneasy as I do if there is no evidence of wine glasses or bottles. Now that I've been forced into making my own bread, I often take it with me. Nobody takes offence, any more than they did in the days of rationing when it was the custom to take one's own marge or butter, sugar and eggs, or egg, whenever invited out to a meal.

It's only a matter of time before the braver and angrier among us start taking our own bread to restaurants. After all, there are plenty of establishments to which we may take our own wine. I see nothing to prevent us taking our own bread as well. The restaurateur can always increase their cover charges to include the loan of a bread knife – if they have one.

FLOUR FOR BREAD

The ideal flours for English bread, and for all yeast doughs, are milled from hard wheat, whereas cake, short pastry and sauce flours are or should be soft-wheat flours. Hard flours have a high gluten content, which makes the dough more elastic and expansive. Soft flour tends to make rather flat bread. (French bread is mostly made from a softish flour because this is the type of wheat mainly grown in France. The French have adapted their bread techniques to their flour.) Nearly all the ordinary white flour sold by grocers in London and the southern area is soft household flour, in the Midlands and the North, where home-baked bread and yeast cakes are still made, the requisite flours are easier to come by.

Whole-wheat flour, stone-ground, 100%, 90% or 85%, whole wheatmeal, can be brought from health-food stores and the like. The first type, 100% wholemeal, is the whole grain of the wheat with nothing removed and nothing added. The 85% and 90% wheatmeal have husk and bran removed and make a lighter and finer loaf. Some whole-food addicts recommend these flours for pastry and sauced. I don't.

The difference between hard gluten flours and ordinary soft household flours becomes apparent as soon as you start handling the dough. The first almost immediately becomes springy and lithe, the latter tends to be sticky and puttyish, although it becomes harder with kneading.

Flours can be mixed. For example, to save continual journeys and the carrying of large parcels of flour bought from a special shop, a mixture of say 4 oz of 100% whole wheatmeal flour and 12 oz of ordinary soft household flour make a quite respectable pale brown loaf, although not such a good one as strong plain or bakers' white flour and 85% or 90% whole wheatmeal flour in the same proportions.

Some of the whole wheatmeal flours on sale in health-food and crank-food shops make a heavy and pudding-like loaf. For that matter, much of the bread sold in these shops is inexpertly made, dry, heavy, calculated to put all but nut-food nuts right off home-made bread for life. Into the bargain, so-called home-made health-food bread is extortionately expensive.

A strong plain flour which makes an excellent loaf is milled by W. & H. Marriage & Sons Ltd., of Chelmsford. This is the bread flour which, together with 85% wheatmeal or 100% wholemeal from the same source, I now use for all my own bread. For other strong white flours, ask for Macdougall's Country Life, Be-Ro plain, Whitworth's Champion, and Hills & Partridge's Golden Age. Hills & Partridge will send their flour by post; their address is Walton Roller Mills, Aylesbury, Buckinghamshire. Another excellent bread flour is Prewett's Millstone plain flour, 81% compost grown, with an added percentage of Manitoba hard wheat flour; it is obtainable in many health and whole-food shops.

There are other respectable wholemeal and wheatmeal flours obtainable from health-food shops and the cranks' counters of department stores. It is simply a question of finding out which suits your own taste.

THE YEAST

In spite of the disappearance of huge numbers of small independent bakeries, a few such shops are still to be found in most towns and suburbs. The bread they sell may not be up to much, but at least most of them will supply yeast if asked. If they won't, it is because, in the concise phrase used by Mr. Clement Freud in an *Observer* cookery article, they are bloody-minded. Or it could be that as, in the case of one of my local Chelsea bakeries, the assistants have made their own bye-laws as to the times of day they will dispense yeast. Or it may depend entirely upon the attitude adopted by the customer.

My own experience is that yeast should be asked for not as a rare favour ("We don't sell yeast, we oblige with it," I have been told by bakeresses) but as a commodity which it is to be taken for granted is sold by a baker as a publican sells beer and as a newsagent sells newspapers.

As opposed to brewers' yeast, which is liquid (and very bitter), bakers' yeast (formerly called German yeast, no doubt because it came from Holland) is compressed yeast. It looks like putty-coloured plasticine. Bakers who make their own bread on the premises will sell yeast – if they sell it at all – in small quantities; from 1 oz upwards. Bakers' yeast is also now sold by some health and whole-food shops.

Yeast can be stored for several days in an airtight box in the refrigerator, so long as it is kept perfectly dry.

It should feel cool and plastic to the touch and smell sweet and alive. The fresher the yeast, the easier it is to make the dough and the better the resulting loaf.

Half an ounce of bakers' yeast will aerate 1 lb to 1½ lb of flour. For a 3 lb batch of dough, use 1 oz of yeast.

Dough made with dried yeast in granules takes a lot longer to rise than dough made with bakers' yeast, and the resulting bread tends to be dry and uninteresting because it lacks the characteristic flavour and smell of yeast. In other words, I find dried yeast unsatisfactory, although many people swear that it's just as good and as easy to work with as bakers' yeast.

THE EQUIPMENT

> A small self-sealing plastic box for the storage of yeast in the refrigerator.
> Scales.
> A cup for mixing the yeast and water.
> A measuring jug.
> A large mixing bowl or bread panshon (a wide earthenware bowl glazed inside) or large wooden bowl.
> A flour-shaker or caster.
> A plastic or rubber or wooden spatula or scraper.
> A clean tea-cloth and a small thick towel.
> Bread tins (2 pint capacity for a loaf made with a pound of flour and a half pint of water). An attractive flat round loaf can be made in a shallow (2 inches deep) French cake tin. I make most of my bread in this type of tin, because I prefer the maximum proportion of crust to crumb. An ordinary round 2 lb cake tin also makes an attractive loaf. A long narrow aluminium tin makes a beautiful loaf, easy for slicing and ideal for sandwiches. It is worth bearing in mind that English bread used to be baked in earthenware pans. If you have no suitable tins, perhaps you have a straightforward earthenware casserole or pie dish which will

serve the purpose. Some people even use ordinary flowerpots, very well rubbed with fat and they make perfectly good loaves. At Easter, I make bread in the fish-shaped moulds traditional to Alsace and Germany.

> A wire grid or cake cooling rack.

AN ENGLISH LOAF

THE BASIC RECIPE

My advice to beginners is to start with the basic recipe for a loaf made with 1 lb of flour, ½ oz of yeast and ½ pint of water, and baked in a 2 pint capacity tin. Only when it is made and cut and pronounced passable or a failure, read the remainder of these notes. Then make another loaf. If after two or three attempts things still don't seem quite right, try one of the variations, or buy one or other of the little books recommended on page 27 and choose another recipe. My recipe suits me and I know that it has suited quite a few complete beginners. That doesn't say it will suit everybody. No recipe ever suits everybody, and this is perhaps more true of bread making and baking than of any other branch of cookery, with the exception of meat roasting.

For a loaf of 85% or 90% whole-wheat flour or plain white flour preferably strong or bakers' flour,[1] you need:

1 lb plain white or wheatmeal flour (or 12 oz white to 4 oz wheatmeal), plus a little flour in a shaker or a bowl for sprinkling on the dough while kneading; ½ oz bakers' yeast; 2 heaped teaspoons of coarse rock or sea salt (more if you like salty bread – I do, and use

---

1 For notes on different types of bread flour see pages 9 and 10.

1 oz per lb of flour); about ½ pint of tepid water; fat for greasing the bread tin.

Put the yeast into a teacup, make it into a cream with 2 or 3 tablespoons of cold or tepid water.

Take off your rings and put them in a safe place.[2]

Put the flour into a big wide bowl, mix well, make a hole in the centre of the flour and pour in the yeast and water paste. Flick the flour over the yeast. Add the water, into which you have stirred the salt until it has dissolved. You may need a little more or a little less than the half pint; this depends on the flour. Mix the dough. This can be done with your hands or with a spatula or long-handled wooden spoon. The mixture should come away fairly smoothly from the bowl, like pastry dough. At this stage, start kneading. (With a small batch of bread, you don't need a board; mixing and kneading can be done in the bowl.) Almost at once, you feel that the dough is beginning to acquire its proper elastic quality. If it is too soft and wet – that is, if you have added too much water – you can dry it by sprinkling it with more flour, but after you have made bread a few times, you won't need to do this because you will get to know just how much water your flour will absorb. Within a few seconds, the dough should be pliable enough to be rolled or folded

---

2 This recipe was originally written for my sister Diana Grey, whose tendency to mislay her engagement ring while cooking has caused many a household drama. In fact it is always wise, when working with dough which may be sticky, to remove any ring other than a plain band.

over on itself in a roughly three-cornered fashion, then to be punched down again. If at this stage the dough is sticky, sprinkle it again with flour. Repeat the folding process three or four times.

Now form it into a large bun shape. Sprinkle it with flour, cover the bowl with a floured tea-cloth (the flour is to prevent the dough sticking to the cloth as it rises), and a small thick towel, folded.

In the winter, I leave my dough for its first rising for one to one and a half hours on top of the stove while the oven is on at No. 1 to 3, 290°-330°F. When the weather is exceptionally cold, increase the oven heat a little.

The dough is sufficiently risen when it has just about doubled in volume.

Butter or grease a 2 pint capacity tin, and sprinkle it with flour. Break down the risen dough. Knead it very thoroughly. Soon it will be like a piece of thick smooth cloth which you can pick up and smack down again on the table or into the bowl. This second kneading is more important than the first. The more you knock the dough about, the better it will be. The object is temporarily to check the action of the yeast. The second kneading for a pound of dough takes a maximum of three minutes. A big batch of dough obviously takes longer.

Advice to owners of electric mixers with dough-mixer attachment: do the kneading by hand until you get used to the process; when you know how it should feel and look, you can make larger batches and use the mixer.

Put the dough into the prepared tin, sprinkling the top with flour (for a wholemeal or half-wholemeal loaf, use wholemeal rather than white flour for this operation – it makes a more attractive crust) and giving it roughly the shape of the tin, which at this stage looks a good deal too big for the amount of dough.

Cover the tin with the floured cloth and towel and return it to a warm place for the dough to rise for the second time. In about 45 minutes to an hour (on top of the stove with the oven alight), the dough should have risen to the top of the tin and is ready to bake.

The airing cupboard and a warm spot close to a boiler are alternatives, and in summer, particularly in steamy weather, the dough can be left covered on the kitchen table without benefit of extra heat.

By this time, have the oven turned on at No. 9, 450°F to 475°F. Put the bread in the centre of the oven. After 15 minutes, turn down the heat to No. 7, 420°F to 440°F. Cook for another 25 to 30 minutes. By now the loaf is slightly shrunk in the tin. Turn it out of the tin upside down on to a wire rack on the kitchen table. With your knuckle, tap the underside of the loaf. If it sounds hollow, like a drum, it is cooked. If it feels soft, it is undercooked. Return it, upside down, to the oven and let it cook for another 10 to 15 minutes with the oven turned down to No. 5, 400°F. An alternative timing, and temperature, is about 50 minutes at No. 7, 420°F to 440°F throughout the whole baking. Where bread is concerned a little too long in the oven is preferable to an undercooked loaf.

Always let the bread cool on a wire rack or grid, so that air circulates round it.

When the loaf is cool, wrap it in a clean cloth or put it in a bread crock or enamelled bin. Plastic boxes soften the crust.

 ## IMPORTANT POINTS TO NOTE

- Adding hot water to yeast will kill it. Cold water doesn't harm yeast. It only makes the rising slightly slower. By the same token, any attempt to speed the rising by leaving the dough in a very hot place will result in the killing of the yeast before the dough goes into the oven.

- Many recipes instruct that you should cream the yeast with sugar and milk. This is to speed the fermenting process. Sugar and milk are both fermenting agents. I find the sugar and milk business unnecessary and undesirable. Water is preferable because even the small quantities of sugar and milk used for creaming the yeast will give a sweet or soft taste to the bread, and that is not my idea of good bread.

- Salt slows up fermentation, so never mix it directly with the yeast. My bread has rather a lot of salt in it, so the dough takes a little longer to rise than is specified in most recipes. Whenever possible, use natural sea or rock salt, finely pounded or ground. Free-running table salt doesn't do much for the taste of bread, and there are those who hold that the chemicals in treated salt can even affect the texture of the loaves. Insufficiency of salt is one of the factors that makes English bread and other yeast goods insipid.

> Bread should always be started in a hot or very hot oven. The loaf rises in the tin in a spectacular manner. After the first 15 minutes the temperature should be reduced or the bread moved to a lower shelf of the oven, because in small domestic ovens the crust tends to burn. Remember that bread bakes best in a falling oven – that is, in gradually decreasing heat. A steamy oven makes the best bread, so it's a help to put a baking tin half-filled with water at the bottom of the oven before you start baking. Leave it there throughout the cooking time.

> Some recipes tell you to gild the loaf with milk and sugar or egg-wash. I don't do this. I don't like a shiny crust. The flour sprinkled on top of the dough during its second rising provides what seems to me the right finish for a home-made loaf. Brushing the loaf with a very strong salt-and-water solution is another way of getting a crisp crust. But it isn't necessary. An extra touch which does produce a most appetising finish to a round loaf is to make a criss-cross of deep incisions in the dough just before it is put into the oven. For this, you need a very sharp knife or a dough cutter (described on page 26). To prevent the blade sticking to the dough, rinse the cutter in very hot water, dry it, make the cuts swiftly.

> Proving and rising mean virtually the same thing. Many bread recipes confuse you by using both terms. Pay no attention. The

term proving in connection with bread really means trying out or proving that the yeast is active.

- › About the preliminary batter or sponge demanded by some bread recipes, this is connected with the note above. Having creamed the yeast, you add a small proportion of the flour and water you are going to use and leave it to ferment. When it starts to work or bubble, after about 20 to 30 minutes, you add it to the main batch of flour, then add the rest of the water and continue in the same way. Bread made from this dough is supposed to be of a better texture than that made in the straightforward manner. I can't say I find all that difference between the two.

- › Comparison of recipes in different books and by different hands reveals many discrepancies and contradictions in times given for the rising and/or proving of the dough, methods of kneading it, and in temperatures suggested for the baking. The discrepancies are due mainly to the large number of possible systems which all lead to approximately the same result. The raising of the dough is really a matter of what suits the individual and his or her habits of life. The process can be slowed down or speeded up if necessary, although over-rapid rising in too high a temperature may result in the killing of the yeast ferment. It is heat rather than cold which is detrimental to yeast. Some recipes recommend leaving the dough to rise in the refrigerator overnight. Others advocate the generation of extra steam by putting the dough into a polythene bag.

> Once you have acquired the most elementary technique of bread-making, it is all very plain sailing. After two or three attempts, the only snag remaining is the washing up. Much of the unnecessary work involved in cleaning the bowls and boards can be eliminated by scraping utensils clean in the first place. Use a rubber, plastic or wooden spatula or dough scraper, and for washing up, a brush rather than a scouring pad. (Scandinavian birch-twig scourers are marvellous for cleaning dough bowls.) After you have made bread a few times, you find that, without realising it, you have acquired the knack of mixing, kneading and raising the dough so that it does not stick to the bowl at all, and the washing up involved becomes negligible.

> To make three small or two larger loaves at a time, the quantities are 3 lb of flour, 1 oz of yeast, approximately 1½ pints of water, and 1½ oz of salt. At first, it is a bit tricky dividing the dough, when ready for putting it in the tins for the second rising, into equal portions. The three loaves are pretty well bound to come out in slightly irregular sizes and textures until you learn to divide the dough (in bakery terms the process is called scaling off) with some degree of accuracy, either by eye or by weighing each piece on the scales, which is what professional bakers are obliged to do because it is a legal offence to sell an underweight or overweight loaf. At home, such considerations are of minor importance.

VARIATIONS ON THE BASIC BREAD RECIPE

A QUICKLY MADE LOAF

Once you know how to make bread, you find that there are many variations on the basic method. You can, for example, get up quite late in the morning and still bake a fresh loaf in time for lunch.

For this method, I use a slightly smaller tin than usual. Tala makes a standard English bread tin of 1¼ pint capacity which holds a small batch of dough made with ¾ lb of flour, ½ oz of yeast, and approximately 8 oz of water.

Procedure: measure out ½ lb of strong plain flour and 4 oz of 85% or 90% wheatmeal. Have your ½ oz of yeast ready, and make it into the usual cream with a little tepid water. Put ¾ oz of pounded *gros sel* into your measuring jug. Cover it with a little *very hot* water so that it dissolves. Add enough tepid water to make up the 8 oz.

Stir the yeast into the flour in the usual way. Add the water, mix the dough very quickly, and do not knead very much.

Put the dough straight into the greased and floured tin. Sprinkle the top with flour, cover it and leave it on top of the stove to rise as usual, but turning your oven a little higher – say to No. 4, 370°F – for about an hour (although the timing can vary from 45 minutes to 1½ hours according to outside climatic conditions), and the dough will have risen to the top of the tin. Turn the oven to No. 9, 450°F-475°F, and when it has been heating for 15 minutes, put the bread in to bake as usual.

Although the quantity of dough is less than for the basic recipe, the baking time is the same or even slightly longer, because a loaf made with only one turn of rising and very little kneading must be very thoroughly baked.

Bread made by this method may have a few holes in the texture. It will be very good while fresh, but will not keep so well as a loaf made by the orthodox method.

Quite often when I come home from my shop in the evening, I find it possible to make, by this method, a quick loaf for a late supper or for next day's sandwich lunch.

A LOAF MADE BY THE EXTRA SLOW METHOD

Sometimes it may be convenient to prolong rather than to hurry the rising of your bread dough. Nothing is easier.

Use the quantities and the mixing method given in the basic recipe, page 16. Instead of leaving the dough in a warm place to rise, put it in a well-covered bowl in a cool spot, for example, near an open window in an unheated room. There are those who advocate the refrigerator for a still slower method. The dough can now be left for 8 to 10 hours. When it is fully risen, it will be unusually light and spongy. It must be very thoroughly knocked down and kneaded for rather longer than usual before it is put, as in the basic method, into the ready-prepared tin to rise for the second time.

By the slowed-up method, the second raising of the dough will also take a little longer than usual. To speed matters – and also to improve the appearance of the loaf – two or three deep slanting cuts can be made in the dough. For this purpose, there is a special utensil called a Scotch scraper or dough-cutter – a wide-bladed curved-edge knife similar to the instrument used by butchers to scrape their meat-chopping blocks. Failing this, the crescent-shaped chopping knife, nowadays sold with a wooden chopping bowl in every kitchen utensil shop, will serve the purpose. For the method of making the cuts see paragraph 2 on page 21.

The rest of the preparations and the baking of this loaf are as for the basic method.

The slowed-up system produces an excellent, well-grown[3] loaf with good keeping qualities.

---

3 The term used by bakers to denote a shapely, professional loaf.

BOOKS ON YEAST COOKERY

Yeast Cookery (revised and combined edition of three booklets formerly called Yeast Cookery, More Yeast Cookery and Yeast Cookery and Home Baking); National Federation of Women's Institutes, 39 Eccleston Street, S.W.1; 15p plus 3p postage.

Succint and lucid explanations of the nature of yeast and its action, of dough mixing, rising and baking. Brief and representative selection of English yeast pastry and tea-bread recipes. Good instructions for bread-making with dried yeast. Less adequate when it comes to continental specialities. The brioche recipe is unhelpful, the authentic pizza recipe in the original edition has been superseded by a version giving a filling which is very odd indeed. Sample instruction: "Kneading. This means folding it (the dough) over on itself and pushing with a firm rocking motion until it becomes smooth and shiny."

Home Baked by George and Cecilia Scurfield; Faber & Faber, 1956; 1971 edition, 45p.

Mr. and Mrs. Scurfield once ran a small home-made bread business from their own kitchen. They were so swamped with orders that they were faced with the choice of turning the business into a full-scale commercial enterprise or giving up altogether. They did the latter and opened a successful kitchen pot shop in Jesus Lane, Cambridge. Their bread book remains for good reasons a steady seller. It is the most reassuring and encouraging of cookery books. A good attempt at a recipe for French bread is included in the Scurfields' book, although I don't recommend beginners to try it. French loaves present technical difficulties hard to overcome when baking in a domestic gas or electric oven.

Sample directions: "The great thing about baking with yeast is the difficulty of failure"; "Don't worry about draughts. It's heat rather than cold that kills the yeast. A croissant dough will double its size overnight in the refrigerator"; "On the whole, it's better to underprove rather than overprove".

Talking about Cakes by Margaret Bates; Pergamon, 1964; £2·00 Miss Bates is the vice-principal of the City of Belfast College of Domestic Science. The recipes for Irish soda bread, griddle bread and other non-yeast-aerated breads are authentic and useful. She gives also sound recipes for white and brown yeast breads, scones and oatcakes.

BREAD ON THE TABLE

FRENCH AND ENGLISH

I am a Frenchman. I cannot eat a meal without bread.

> Andre L. Simon, founder of the Wine and Food Society, upon sitting down at a table upon which no bread was in evidence.

To bring home in a simplified way the extent to which any meal in the authentic French tradition relies upon the presence of bread in the background, in the foreground, in the hand of the diner, on the plate, on the table, I have drawn up the following short list of dishes and foods which it would be unthinkable to a Frenchman, to serve or eat without bread:

- All pâtés; i.e. bread as opposed to the toast customary in England; and it is unusual for the French to serve butter with pâtés.
- Sardines; illogically, given the rich oil content of sardines, butter is obligatory; lemon is usual.
- Anchovies. Pepper, coarsely milled, is obligatory.
- Egg mayonaise and all kindred dishes.
- Olives.

- All first course salads, simple or compound.
- All crudités or raw vegetable hors d'oeuvre.
- All charcuterie or pork butchers' products; i.e. cured sausage, raw ham, cooked ham, hot or cold meat salads, rillettes (potted pork), brawn, tongue, galantines.
- All soups, of whatever nature, even if there is already bread in the soup as in *soupe à l'oignon*.
- All sausage dishes, even if there is potato purée as part of the dish. (There is no bread in the composition of French sausages as there is and always has been, in our own.)
- All egg dishes, most particularly any form of fried eggs or *oeufs sur le plat*, and plain boiled eggs.
- All dishes of meat, fish, poultry or game, including grills, served with a sauce, white or brown, pink or green, whether made with a stock, wine, cream, olive oil or eggs, separately or together.
- All stews, ragoûts, daubes, fricassées, in fact all dishes with a sauce, thick or thin, creamy or liquid, even if there are fried bread croûtons, which often there are, served as part of the dish.

As the cheese course is reached, the almost continual process of bread breaking and munching inseparable from French meals comes to an end. Cheese is one of the extremely few non-sweet foods with which, to the French, bread is not a pre-requisite.

Now for the English dishes and foods with which bread is obligatory or traditionally associated. The list cannot be drawn up on the same lines as that relating to French eating habits. Our own traditions are so totally different that I can think, offhand, of one legendary combination, and one only, in which the absence of a hunk of plain and simple bread would be glaringly obvious to the smallest child: it is the bandana handkerchief knotted in Dick Whittington style from which bread and cheese are inseparable and indivisible. In other words if a meat pie and a choc bar came out of that bundle, something would be very wrong indeed.

For the rest, the following are associated with bread in our speech if not in our lives:

> Butter
> Jam
> Water
> Milk
> Scrape
> Cheese

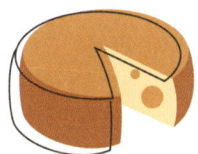

Biscuits are equally accepted, although not by me, as belonging to cheese. But whereas we say bread and cheese with equal emphasis on both commodities, the biscuits take secondary place. Cheese and biscuits, not biscuits and cheese. A glance at any British Railways menu will confirm this curious linguistic quirk.

The following foods are those which would not be accepted without bread, but it must be brown in colour and butter must be spread upon it:

› Oysters
› Smoked salmon

We have invented – or evolved – at least four national specialities based on bread:

› Sauce
› Bread and butter pudding
› Summer pudding
› Sandwiches

And a couple on bread and cheese:

› Welsh rarebit
› Cheese pudding

I don't know who invented restaurateurs' toast, that triangle of damp blanket which is served with the pâté – and with breakfast – in every English hotel and restaurant. This substance is now becoming popular in France. It is listed on French menus as toast whereas real French toast is called *pain grillé* or grilled bread, which is just what it is, or used to be.

DRIED HERBS, AROMATICS AND CONDIMENTS

ELIZABETH DAVID

Published in 2023 by
Grub Street
4 Rainham Close
London
SW11 6SS

Email: food@grubstreet.co.uk
Twitter: @grub_street
Facebook: Grub Street Publishing
Instagram: grubstreetpublishinguk
Web: www.grubstreet.co.uk

ISBN 978-1-911667-08-7

Printed and bound by Print Best, Estonia

Publishers note: The four booklets which constitute this set were first published by Elizabeth David Ltd for sale in her shop Kitchen Utensils, 46 Bourne Street, London SW1 in 1968 and 1969. They are reissued using the original texts which have not been updated.

CONTENTS

HOW TO STORE AND USE

Herbs grown on the hills of Provence, dried naturally, and packaged on the stalk or in whole leaf form retain their potent scents and flavouring qualities to a very high degree. Since each herb is readily recognisable by its characteristic appearance as well as by its scent, identification and storage present no problems. Simply transfer the herbs from their packets to stoppered glass jars, very small ones for leaf herbs, medium size for bay leaves, rosemary and thyme on the stalk. For fennel stalks, space-saving Porosan or polythene bags can be used instead of jars.

BOUQUET GARNI

BOUQUET GARNI I

To make the bouquet garni or faggot of herbs required in so many meat, game and poultry recipes, simply tie together a couple of whole bay leaves, a sprig or two of dried thyme on the stalk, a few fresh parsley stalks, and, for certain dishes such as daubes of beef, a strip of orange peel and a piece of celery. For fish dishes make the bouquet of fennel stalks, lemon peel and bay leaves. Leave a long string on the little bunch so that it can be easily extracted from the pot when cooking is completed.

In the old farmhouse and country cooking of Burgundy, Provence and the Languedoc the bunch of thyme and bay leaves, minus the parsley and the string is sometimes presented on the serving dish with the meat, a little touch which makes a most inviting decoration.

BOUQUET GARNI 2

To make a bouquet of herbs in leaf form (for those who do not care to find the little leaves in their soup or stew) put a teaspoon of mixed basil, marjoram, thyme and savory, with a crumbled bay leaf, in a 4" square of muslin. Add three or four whole peppercorns and, if you like, a peeled clove of garlic crushed with a knife. Tie the little bundle with thread, discard it when the dish is cooked.

For chicken and fish dishes, vary the flavouring by using tarragon or fennel instead of the mixed herbs; for pork and game dishes add crushed juniper berries to the mixture.

Either of the above methods gives results so superior to the anonymous, slightly musty-smelling sachets or so-called bouquet garnis of commerce that it is really worthwhile taking the scarcely noticeable extra trouble. Personally I find the little ritual of preparing herb bouquets one of the minor pleasures of cooking. Nothing would persuade me to relinquish it in favour of a bought bouquet made up in a factory.

DRIED HERBS AS AROMATIC FLAVOURINGS

BASIL (BASILIC)

Crumble a few leaves into freshly made tomato soups and sauces, onion and tomato fillings for Provençal *pissaladière*, aubergines and courgettes stewed in olive oil, white haricot bean and chickpea soups and salads, Italian minestrone and other mixed vegetable soups.

The best way to use dried basil, and indeed all dried herbs, for flavouring uncooked dishes such as salads, is to warm them for a couple of minutes in a low oven, and then crumble the leaves. The full aromas of dried herbs (and of many spices) do not develop until they have been subjected to heat.

In England basil was once the accepted flavouring for sausages and for turtle soup. It also combines uncommonly well with lobster, prawns, and shell fish soups.

BAY LEAVES (LAURIER)

In French cooking bay leaves make a beautiful and almost ritual decoration for the top of a *pâté de campagne*. One or two whole leaves are laid upon the top of the mixture before the pâté is put into the oven. To prevent the leaves curling during cooking, and also to prevent the pâté from overbrowning, press foil or grease-proof paper over the pâté until 15 or 20 minutes before the end of cooking time.

Italian cooks use a compound of chopped onion, celery leaves, garlic, tomato and crumbled bay leaves, all fried in olive oil, to make the mixture called *soffritto* which is the aromatic basis of a hundred and one Italian soups, stews and sauces.

FENNEL (FENOUIL)

A bundle of tinder-dry fennel stalks is one of two essential components of the famous *grillade au fenouil* of the Mediterranean coast of Provence – the other essential, the fish itself, should be sea bass (*loup de mer*) or alternatively a big fat red mullet. The grilled fish is placed on a grid over the fennel stalks and armagnac or brandy is set ablaze and poured over the fennel. As it burns the fennel envelops the fish with aromatic scents. Pork chops or chicken halves cooked in much the same way make delicious and sweet-smelling dishes. The recipes on pages 20 and 23 will provide ideas.

MARJORAM (MARJOLAINE)

This is the herb for flavouring roast lamb and grilled lamb kebabs. A sprinkling of marjoram also goes into pizza fillings, veal and poultry stuffings and Greek moussaka. *Origano*, the Italian word for marjoram, is simply a corruption of *origanum,* the botanical name for all marjorams. Italian cooks use marjoram in countless ravioli and cannelloni stuffings, pasta sauces, and the delicate little minced lamb or veal rissoles called *polpette* or *polpettine*.

In Provence marjoram is much used in civets of rabbit and also in rice stuffings for courgettes, aubergines, tomatoes and sweet peppers. It is less well known that marjoram is a wonderful herb for flavouring white fish such as hake, cod and halibut. The marjoram of Provence is powerfully aromatic and spicy. A little goes a long way.

ROSEMARY (ROMARIN)

"Poor Ophelia" wrote Marcel Boulestin, "she thought rosemary was for remembrance. It is for cooking veal."

I find that rosemary is best used rather as are fennel stalks: placed underneath or around chicken, veal, pork or lamb to be roasted or grilled. When the rosemary has given out its scent, discard it. The leaves are spiky and acrid and should not be allowed to find their way into sauces or stocks nor on to anyone's plate.

Most Italian cooks are reckless in their use of rosemary, stuffing it regardless into pork, lamb and veal joints, but once in Capri I saw an old woman dipping a long sprig of rosemary into olive oil and using it to baste the fish she was grilling over an open fire. A very proper approach to this potent herb.

Like fennel stalks, rosemary can be strewn on a charcoal fire for grilling steak, chops, kebabs or fish and will give out a wonderful scent as the food cooks.

SAVORY (SARRIETTE)

This rather peppery herb makes an excellent flavouring for dried vegetables such as white haricot beans, lentils, and chick peas. Mixed with onion stuffings for duck, pork and goose, savory gives a more subtle flavour than sage.

Claire Loewenfeld, founder of the Chiltern Herb Farm and author of *Herbs for Health and Cookery*, tells us that savory can be used almost as a spice and can replace both salt and pepper. It is therefore especially recommended to those on a salt-free diet.

The needly-looking little leaves which coat the picturesque goat's milk and ewe's milk cheeses of upper Provence, although sometimes mistaken for rosemary, are in fact the dried leaves of *sarriette* or *poivre d'ane* as savory is called in Provence, Home-made milk or cream cheeses can be treated in much the same way. Simply sprinkle a plate with warmed, crumbled dried savory and turn the cheese in it until both sides are just speckled with the little leaves. Store for a couple of days before eating.

Savory, like rosemary, is a herb to be used sparingly.

TARRAGON (ESTRAGON)

As with basil, tarragon in its dried form can never be more than a substitute for the fresh herb at its best. Fresh tarragon at its best is however a rarity, and the season is short. During the winter and spring good quality dried tarragon is a valuable standby. One of the best ways to use it is in tarragon butter (the recipe is on page 23) for serving with grilled steak, for flavouring a roasting chicken, for adding to Bearnaise sauce, to *eggs en cocotte* with cream and to omelettes.

The Chiltern Herb Farm true French tarragon, grown and dried in the most propitious conditions, retains the fresh tarragon flavour to a very high degree. Remember that as with all dried herbs, heat develops and brings out the scent and flavour.

THYME (THYM)

Wild thyme from the hills of Provence, dried by the sun before it is picked, retains its aromatic qualities longer than any other herb. Use it to scent roast lamb, pork, veal, grilled chicken, beef and wine stews, baked or grilled fish. A sprig or two of dried wild thyme stored in a jar with black olives in oil or brine gives the olives a delicious scent. Provence wild thyme on the stalk is, to me, the most beloved and necessary of all dried herbs.

AROMATICS AND CONDIMENTS

DIJON MUSTARD

When mustard is to be used to flavour a sauce or mayonnaise the strong yellow variety is the best choice. A brown mustard distorts the colour, and is also very often a sweetened or over-spiced compound lacking the true mustard flavour.

When used to flavour cooked sauces, Dijon mustard should be added only a minute or two before the sauce is ready. Heat quickly dissipates the flavour and pungency. In dishes such as cheese soufflés, where longer cooking is unavoidable, use just that much more mustard than you think necessary.

SAFFRON

To flavour and colour a risotto, a paella, or a pilaff for four people infuse a few saffron filaments (it is impossible to count them: use about as many as would spread thinly on a sixpence) in a little coffee cup of hot stock or water. Leave for about 20 minutes, until the liquid is stained a brilliant orange. Strain off the liquid into the rice dish. This operation is usually carried out when the risotto or paella is already nearly cooked. To speed the infusing process, warm the saffron in a low oven for five minutes and crumble the filaments before pouring the stock over them.

Saffron is an essential flavouring of bouillabaisse and of many fish soups and broths. For soups, the whole saffron filaments are put into the stock pot with all the other aromatics such as fennel stalks, garlic, celery, peppercorns, bay leaves; all are strained off before the final stages of cooking. Except to serious saffron addicts, it is not entirely welcome to find the whole filaments in the soup.

Saffron is so light and so valuable that it is sold by the grain. There are 437 grains to the ounce, and 5 grains are sufficient to flavour and colour three to four pounds of rice.

JUNIPER BERRIES

It was the highly aromatic and pungent berry of the juniper, in Latin *ginepro,* which gave its name to gin and is the most important of the aromatics which go to make up its characteristic flavour.

Juniper berries also make a wonderful seasoning for pâtés, stuffings for small game birds, and pork dishes. The dried berries should be used in small quantities and should always be crushed in a mortar or chopping bowl before they are added to a pâté mixture or a stuffing, or mixed with salt, olive oil and garlic as a seasoning for pork chops. Juniper berries are also used to flavour wine marinades for venison and mutton, in brines for hams and salt pork, and in the mixture for curing dry-spiced beef.

An interesting recipe for a dish of veal kidneys called *rognons à la liégoise* is given by Ambrose Heath in *Good Food*. The kidneys are rapidly cooked in butter, and just before they are ready to serve you throw in a few crushed juniper berries, then a wineglassful of gin warmed in a ladle, ignited, and poured blazing over the kidneys. This, adds the author, is 'quite wonderful'. The gin, I should add, gives a terrific blaze and a most excellent flavour. It is a spirit which could be used more often in the kitchen.

Stored in a stoppered glass jar, dried juniper berries will keep for years.

VANILLA BEANS

The following recipe for a vanilla ice-cream mixture from *Gunter's Modern Confectioner* (1861) gives some idea of the lavish way in which this powerfully scented and highly prized bean was used before the discovery of synthetic essence:

"Chop up half an ounce of vanilla, pound it very fine in a metal mortar. Take five or six ounces of sugar, and add it by degrees to the vanilla, and pound together. When done, put this into a pint of fresh cream, with the yolks of seven or eight eggs, make hot over a fire, but do not boil. Strain through a sieve. When sufficiently cool put it in the freezing pot and work it well."

To make vanilla sugar for flavouring sweet pastry and fruit dishes, it is not really necessary to pound the vanilla beans. Simply cut one or two into halves or quarters, store these in a jar of caster sugar. After a few days the sugar will be strongly scented.

To make a vanilla-flavoured custard or cream put a whole bean into the milk, egg and sugar mixture. Extract it when the custard is thickened and cooled. The vanilla bean can be used many times. Dry it in the plate drawer of the oven and return it to the caster sugar jar.

Do not try to strain out the tiny black specks left by the vanilla bean after cooking. They are the visible signs of the authenticity of flavouring in a vanilla ice cream, custard or soufflé.

A piece of vanilla bean baked with sliced apples, whole plums or apricots gives the fruit an extraordinary and haunting scent.

RECIPES

SIMPLE FISH STOCK

The making of a broth, stock or *court bouillon* for fish sauces is a simple, quick and straightforward process. The difference effected to the finished dish far outweighs the small amount of extra trouble involved.

All you have to do is put the trimmings, head and carcase of the fish – if it is a large one such as brill or John Dory ask the fishmonger to break it up for you – into a saucepan with a peeled onion, a little slice of lemon, some sprigs of tarragon or a few fennel stalks, a bay leaf or two, a couple of tablespoons of wine vinegar or four of white wine, and about a teaspoon of salt. You then pour in enough cold water just to cover the contents. Bring it to simmering point and then allow about 25 minutes' very gentle cooking.

Now strain the stock and measure off the quantity you need for the recipe. Most commonly, a fish stock is used as a basis for a cream sauce for fillets of sole, brill or John Dory, or for gratins of turbot, skate, hake or shellfish.

The same stock with the addition of a tomato or two, a few saffron filaments, shells and heads of prawns or shrimps, a sliced carrot, a leek, a piece of celery – in fact any flavouring vegetables you have to hand – also makes the basis of any number of fish soups.

Never let fish stock boil fiercely or for a prolonged period or you may get that slightly acrid taste from the bones and skin of the fish (although of course much depends on the variety of fish you are cooking) which characterises a carelessly-made fish soup or sauce. You can always obtain a more concentrated flavour by reducing the stock after it has been strained.

TUSCAN BEAN SOUP

Put ½ lb of the white haricots known as cannellini beans, or of pink borlotti beans (both are to be found at Italian delicatessen shops), to soak in cold water. Leave them overnight.

Next day put the drained beans into a *fagiolara* (a flask-shaped Tuscan earthenware bean jar) or into a tall soup marmite or stock pot. Cover them with approximately 3 pints of fresh cold water. Add three or four bay leaves, a teaspoon of dried savory or basil leaves (Tuscan cooks use sage. I find it too overpowering), 3 tablespoons of fruity olive oil.

Cook the beans, covered, over moderate heat for about two hours. Now add a tablespoon of salt and continue cooking for another 20 to 30 minutes, until the beans are quite soft.

Now sieve half the beans only, with about half the liquid, through the mouli-légumes (or purée them in the electric blender, but not for long enough to get an unattractive electric-mixer-foam on the top); mix the purée with the rest of the beans, add a good fistful of parsley, coarsley chopped with a clove or two of garlic, and reheat the soup. Before serving stir in a ladleful of fruity olive oil and the juice of a lemon.

In each soup plate or bowl have ready a slice of coarse country bread – or the nearest you can get to such a commodity – rubbed with garlic and sprinkled with olive oil.

A half pound of beans should make enough soup for four.

PRAWN PASTE

An excellent little first course dish for three to four people.
½ lb peeled cooked prawns; 4-6 teaspoonsful of olive oil; seasonings of dried basil, cayenne pepper, and the juice of a fresh lime or lemon. For a more spiced flavour add a saltspoon of crushed coriander or cumin seed.

Mash or pound the prawns to a paste. Very gradually, add the olive oil. Season with cayenne pepper and about a half teaspoonful of dried basil warmed in the oven and finely crumbled. Add the strained juice of half a lemon or of a whole fresh lime (when available, the lime is much the better choice). When the mixture is smooth, and is seasoned to your satisfaction – salt may or may not be necessary, that depends upon how much has already been cooked with the prawns – pack it into a little jar or terrine. Cover and store in the refrigerator. Serve chilled, with hot thin toast. Do not attempt to store for more than a couple of days.

If using freshly boiled prawns in the shell, allow approximately 1½ pints gross measure. The shells and heads will make the basis of a good shellfish soup.

N.B. In an electric blender or automatic chopper the prawns and olive oil can be mashed to a paste in a couple of minutes.

PORK CHOPS BAKED WITH AROMATIC HERBS

This dish is a good example of one in which the scent of aromatic herbs make the whole difference; it should provide ideas for many others of the same sort.

For two people buy a couple of nice thick chops without rind. Score the meat lightly on each side. Cut a peeled clove of garlic in half and rub the meat with the cut surface. Press in salt and a little freshly milled black pepper. Coat each side of both chops with olive oil. In a baking dish arrange half a dozen twigs of wild thyme, several whole bay leaves and a dozen fennel stalks. On top put the chops. If you have time, make these preparations an hour or so in advance, or in the morning for the evening, so that the herbs and seasonings have already scented the meat before cooking starts. Put the dish under the grill, and let the chops brown lightly on each side. Now cover the dish with oiled paper or foil and transfer it to a low oven, gas No. 3, 330 deg. F., and leave for 40 to 50 minutes.

Finally, pour off into a bowl any excess fat which has come from the meat during cooking. Serve the chops as they are, in their cooking dish, herbs and all.

A simple enough dish, deliciously flavoured; and needing no other accompaniment than a green salad, or a few sliced tomatoes dressed with oil and sprinkled with onion and parsley.

STEAK AU POIVRE

Allow a scant half teaspoon each of whole black and whole white peppercorns for each fillet or entrecote steak. Other ingredients are garlic, olive oil, salt, parsley or tarragon butter.

Crush the peppercorns, not too finely, in a mortar. Rub each steak with a cut clove of garlic and about one tablespoon of olive oil. Coat each steak with its portion of crushed peppercorns. Leave the meat for an hour or two – or overnight – to imbibe the flavours.

Immediately before cooking, sprinkle with coarse salt.

The steaks can be dry-fried in a cast-iron pan or cooked on a top-of-the-stove grilling device such as the ridged cast-iron Monogrill made by Le Creuset. In either case no extra fat is needed, and the pan or grill should be made very hot before the steaks are put on to cook. Once the meat is seared on both sides, decrease the heat rapidly. A thick fillet of approximately 7 oz weight will take about 7 minutes to cook to the medium rare stage, and should be turned frequently, with tongs, NOT WITH A FORK, during cooking.

Have ready a hot serving dish, the parsley or tarragon butter, and whatever vegetable or salad is to accompany the steak. Serve immediately. A grilled steak should no more be kept waiting than should a soufflé or an omelette.

The quantity of pepper suggested in this recipe is ample for most people, but can be increased or decreased according to taste. French restaurant cooks tend to overdo the pepper on steak au poivre to the point where their victims choke on the very first mouthful.

TARRAGON BUTTER

Work together 2 oz of butter, 2 teaspoons of Chiltern Herb Farm dried tarragon, a squeeze of lemon juice and a scrap of freshly milled black pepper. Stored in a small covered jar in the refrigerator, tarragon butter will keep several days, so it is often worth making double quantities.

CHICKEN POT ROASTED WITH FENNEL AND HAM

For a 3½ lb roasting chicken (2¾ lb dressed and drawn weight) the other ingredients are a half dozen each of dried fennel stalks and whole bay leaves; 4 to 6 oz mild, cooked ham in one piece; 2 or 3 garlic cloves; a strip of lemon peel; 2 oz butter; a half dozen whole black peppercorns. Optionally, 4 tablespoons of brandy.

Tie the fennel stalks and bay leaves into a bunch. Put them into an earthenware or cast-iron cocotte or pot. On top put the chicken (lying on its side) stuffed with the peeled garlic cloves, the strip of lemon peel and the ham cut into finger-thick strips and liberally sprinkled with coarsely crushed black peppercorns (no salt). Add the butter in small pieces.

Cover the pot, put it low down into a medium hot oven, gas No. 5, 400 deg. F. Leave for 45 minutes. Now turn the chicken, basting it with the butter, and return it to the oven. Cook for another 45 to 50 minutes.

Now uncover the pot, turn the chicken breast upwards and leave it to brown in the oven for 10 to 15 minutes.

To give the dish a spectacular finish, and to bring out to their full extent the scents and flavours of the aromatic herbs, transfer the pot to mild heat on top of the stove. Pour the brandy into a ladle, warm it, ignite it, pour it flaming over the chicken, rotate the pan so that the flames spread. After they have died down transfer the chicken to an ovenproof serving dish but leave the juices in the casserole to cook and mature for another 3 or 4 minutes. Pour them off into a sauceboat.

For serving, arrange the fennel stalks and bay leaves on the dish with the chicken.

Make sure, when the chicken is carved, that everybody has a share of the little strips of ham from the inside of the bird.

Basically, this is a dish of the old-fashioned country cooking of Tuscany. The final blaze of brandy is a modern flourish.

PARSLEY AND LEMON STUFFING FOR A CHRISTMAS TURKEY OR CAPON

For a 10 to 12 lb turkey stuffing: ½ lb dried breadcrumbs; 2 large lemons; 6 tablespoonful of finely chopped parsley; one teaspoonful of dried marjoram; 1 lb unsalted butter; 3 whole eggs; salt, freshly milled pepper.

To prepare the breadcrumbs for the stuffing, cut the crusts from a sliced white loaf, dry the slices on a baking sheet in a low oven until they are quite brittle, but not coloured.

Pound them to crumbs with a rolling pin, or in the electric blender.

To make the stuffing, mix the breadcrumbs with the parsley (be sure to wash it before chopping it), add the marjoram, the grated peel of the two lemons and the strained juice of one. Beat in the eggs, then the softened butter. Season very lightly. Stuff the bird (body and crop) and secure the flaps with small metal skewers, so that the stuffing will not burst out during cooking.

For a 6 to 7 lb capon, reduce the quantities by one third.

TO COOK THE TURKEY

Rub the bird with ¼ lb of butter, putting lumps between the thighs and body. Wrap the bird in cooking foil, also lavishly buttered. Stand the parcel, the turkey lying on its side, on a rack in a baking tin and place it low down in the oven preheated to very moderate (gas No. 3, 330 deg. F.). A 10-12 lb bird takes 2¾ to 3 hours to cook.

At half time turn the bird over, and 30 minutes before time is up, take away the foil and turn the bird breast upwards so that it will brown. Over it pour a little glass of white wine or vermouth. Mingling with the buttery juices in the pan, this will produce a most delicious little extra sauce.

A capon can be cooked in exactly the same way, allowing approximately 2 hours cooking time.

GIBLET GRAVY

The giblet gravy is best started off a day ahead of time. Put the giblets (keep the liver for another dish) with 2 carrots, one onion, a small glass of white wine or vermouth, a bouquet of herbs, ½ lb of stewing veal, and two halved and grilled tomatoes into a small soup pot. Set over a low flame without other liquid. Let the wine cook and all the ingredients take colour before adding salt and enough water to cover. Transfer the pot, covered, to a very low oven (perhaps at the same time as the bread for the stuffing is drying) for about 2 hours. Return it to the oven again, if there is room, while the turkey is cooking. At about the same time as you open the oven to take the foil off the turkey, remove the giblet stock, strain it, transfer it to a saucepan and keep it ready on the top of the stove for the final heating up.

ANGEVIN SALAD

This is a lovely salad to serve after a roast turkey or capon.

Hearts of two lettuces or of two curly endives or Batavian endives; ½ lb Gruyère or Emmenthal cheese; olive oil and wine vinegar for the dressing.

The salad must be fresh and crisp. Wash and dry it well ahead of time. With it in the bowl mix the Gruyère or Emmenthal (the latter is the one with the large holes, whereas the real Gruyère has very small ones) cut into tiny cubes. Add the dressing, made from 6 tablespoonsful of olive oil to a teaspoonful or two at most of vinegar, at the last minute.

Instead of olive oil, the light walnut oil of Touraine can be used for the dressing. Combined with the cheese it makes a beautiful and interesting mixture.

OXFORD BRAWN SAUCE

Put two tablespoons of soft, dark brown sugar into a bowl. Stir in 2 teaspoons of strong yellow Dijon mustard. Add ½ a teaspoon each of freshly milled black pepper and salt.

Now add, gradually, stirring all the time, 6 tablespoons of olive oil. Finally, add two tablespoons of wine vinegar. The sauce should be thick and translucent, looking rather like dark honey.

Except that I have reduced the amount of vinegar, this recipe is in all essentials the one given by Eliza Acton in her famous *Modern Cookery* of 1845. It is a splendid sauce to eat with cold spiced beef as well as with brawn.

CUMBERLAND SAUCE

This best of all sauces for cold meat – ham, pressed beef, tongue, venison, boar's head or pork brawn – can be made in small quantities and in a quick and economical way as follows:

With a potato parer cut the rind, very thinly, from two large oranges. Slice this into match-stick strips. Plunge them into boiling water and let them boil 5 minutes. Strain them.

Put them in a bowl with 4 tablespoons of redcurrant jelly, a heaped teaspoon of yellow Dijon mustard, a little freshly milled pepper, a pinch of salt.

Place this bowl over a saucepan of water, and heat, stirring all the time, until the jelly is melted and the mustard smooth. Now add 4 tablespoons of medium tawny port. Stir and cook another 5 minutes. Serve cold. There will be enough for four.

Made in double or triple quantities this sauce can be stored in covered jars and will keep for several weeks.

N.B. On no account should cornflour, gelatine or any other stiffening be added to Cumberland sauce. The mixture thickens as it cools, and the sauce is invariably served cold, even with a hot ham or tongue.

VANILLA-FLAVOURED SYRUP

To make a vanilla-flavoured syrup in which to bake or to poach pears, peaches, apricots or apples, proportions are 6 oz of caster sugar to ¼ pint of water and one whole vanilla bean.

Put all the ingredients in a heavy aluminium or untinned copper saucepan. Set it over moderate heat. When the sugar has dissolved, increase the heat and let the mixture boil for approximately 7 minutes. Let the syrup cool before the fruit is put in to cook.

The proportions given will make a syrup of approximately 30 degrees Beaume, which is also the required density for the syrup to mix with a fruit purée for a sorbet or water ice.

MELON COMPOTE

Cut the flesh of a honeydew melon into cubes, put them into a heat-resistant china or glass bowl. Pour over them enough boiling syrup, made as described above, to cover the melon. Leave for several hours so that the melon imbibes the syrup.

Next day strain off the syrup, boil it again for five minutes, pour it back over the melon.

Serve very cold.

The flavour and texture of a rather uninteresting melon are enormously improved by this treatment.

TOMATO PRESERVE

However freakish it may sound, this is a delicate and beautiful preserve. It was evidently one of Marcel Boulestin's favourite sweetmeats; a recipe for tomato jam or preserve appears in every one of his cookery books.

2 lb very ripe and sweet tomatoes, 2 lb sugar, a vanilla bean, ½ pint of water.

In a wide preserving pan boil the sugar and water to a syrup. Add the tomatoes, skinned and sliced. Boil steadily stirring fairly often for about 35 minutes. Put in the vanilla bean (vanilla essence will not do). Cook for, approximately, 10 to 15 minutes longer or until setting point is reached. Remove the vanilla pod, skim the jam, and let it cool for a few minutes before turning it into small jars.

Tomato jam is particularly good when eaten in the French way, as a sweet, with fresh cream cheese or plain pouring cream.

To skin tomatoes put them in a big heat-resistant bowl. Cover them with boiling water. Leave for a couple of minutes. The skins can then easily be peeled off.

INDEX OF RECIPES